THE CORPORATE CRUSH

Success Often Comes When Leadership Shift from *Ego-Drive* to *Co-Drive*

SANTOSH KUMAR SINGH

Contents

Contents

About Author

"Santosh Singh is a seasoned banking and finance professional with over 25 years of experience in the industry. Having worked with leading banks, NBFCs, and corporate entities, Santosh has developed a deep understanding of the intricacies of the financial sector & corporate issues.

A prolific writer, Santosh has previously authored a book named "One Step In Corporate Sphere "that showcased his expertise and insights into the world of corporate. His writing is informed by his extensive experience and provides valuable perspectives on the complex issues facing the industry & way to deal with it.

With a career spanning over two and a half decades, Santosh has established himself as a respected voice in the banking, finance & corporate community. His latest work promises to offer fresh insights and expertise, drawing on his vast experience and knowledge of Work life balance, corporate challenges, & transformation of work culture.

About Book

With over 25 years of experience in the industry, I have witnessed firsthand the challenges and opportunities that arise in this dynamic landscape, through this book, I hope to share my experiences, successes, and learnings.

In today's fast-paced corporate world, the stakes are high, and the expectations are even higher. As a manager, you will face numerous challenges, threats, and opportunities that will test your mettle. You will need to navigate complex team dynamics, set ambitious goals, and maintain a delicate work-life balance.

This book is designed to be your trusted companion on this journey. It is packed with practical advice, real-world examples, and actionable tips to help you overcome the obstacles and seize the opportunities that come with being a first-time manager.

Through these pages, you will learn how to:

- Identify and overcome the common challenges that first-time managers face
- Recognize and mitigate the threats that can derail your team's progress
- Capitalize on the opportunities that can propel your team to success
- Build and lead high-performing teams that are motivated, engaged, and productive
- Set and achieve ambitious goals that align with your organization's vision
- Maintain a healthy work-life balance that nourishes your mind, body, and spirit

This is not just a theoretical guide; it is a practical handbook that draws on my own experiences as a corporate leader, as well as the insights and expertise of other seasoned managers.

So, if you are ready to take the leap and become a successful first-time manager, then my effort is for you. Let's get started!

Purpose of the Book

All revenue generated from this book will be dedicated towards supporting Employee Mental Health initiatives, this commitment reflects our dedication to prioritizing the well-being of our workforce.

By investing in Mental Health, we aim to foster a Healthier, Happier and more Resilient Team.

"Fuel Your Passion"
(Without Energy, Talent Sits Idle)

Just because we are talented doesn't mean we will be successful, talent alone is not enough The energy you bring on the table made the difference.

You can have all the talent in the world, but without the right energy, enthusiasm, and commitment, it won't take you very far.

We must have seen such people at some point in our professional career who seem to have it all intelligence, skills, experience but yet they struggle to make progress.

On the other side, we've also seen people with average talent but incredible drive who outperform just because of Positive Energy and its It drives consistency, creativity, and resilience. It makes you stand out—not just for what you know, but for how you show up.

Our Energy Set Out Tone- For example, we are having a meeting with our team about a new policy or a new task, so at that time you have 2 options.

First tell us directly what we have to tell or the topic on which we have to discuss and give orders that we have to do it.

And the second option is that we have to show our excitement and keep the team engaged, so that the team can discuss their ideas freely and came out as a Team.

Success isn't a straight line. There will be days when motivation turns low, when challenges seem crushing, when nothing seems to be working. That's when energy becomes your greatest asset.

The people who keep going, who pivot instead of quitting, who learn instead of getting discouraged—they are the ones who make it.

When you approach your work with passion, doors start to open, People take notice. They remember your enthusiasm, your drive, and your attitude. They want to collaborate with you, invest in you, and elevate you to greater heights.

Your talent is a gift, but your energy is your superpower, use it wisely and keep going on.

"Focus on Possibility"

True leaders inspire by seeing possibilities, not problems and the Accidental Leaders who always seemed to focus on what could go wrong.

The True leaders whether in business, community, or life—don't ignore challenges, but they refuse to be defined by them, they shift the focus from boundaries to resolutions, from barriers to revolutions.

You can choose to see possibilities instead of problems and that one mindset shift can transform your career, your leadership, and your impact.

Accidental leaders always look for faults in their team members. They think that all the faults are in the team members only, they always speak about problem instead for solution, actually such leaders not capable self to find out solution, they just know about shouting from sitting Cabin and only attitude is Hire and Fire.

True Leader sees the same market recession, but they focus on what can be done. They explore new strategies, upskill their team, and find innovative ways to stay ahead. Instead of being paralyzed by uncertainty, they adapt, innovate, and inspire and that's actually worked.

leadership isn't about having all the answers. It's about having the mindset to keep moving forward even when things look uncertain. Leaders who focus on possibilities instead of problems create energy, and energy is what drives success.

True Leaders always ask what can we do instead of why is this happening, they always work with concept of How instead Why.

People don't just follow leaders for their strategies—they follow them for their belief in the future.

Problems are temporary. True Leaders with a possibility mindset play the long game, they make decisions based on growth, not fear.

"When Life Gives You Lemons, Make Lemonade"

(A positive attitude transforms obstacles into opportunities)

You all must have experienced that life does not always go according to plan, we all set a goal, make a detailed plan and work hard according to that plan, but somewhere we get frustrated and disappointed when the work does not go according to the plan, many obstacles arise and challenges arise in many ways and in these moments that our attitude makes all the difference.

Difficulties are unavoidable. No one gets through life without difficulties, and no career path is perfectly smooth. Some days, it feels like everything is working against you, opportunities slip away, and plans fall apart. It's tempting to give in to negativity, but here's the truth your attitude determines your outcome.

When you approach challenges with a positive attitude, you stop seeing difficulties as roadblocks and start seeing them as redirections.

Instead of asking, "Why is this happening to me?" ask, "What is this trying to teach me that's a Positive Attitude, please remember. Every great success story is filled with moments of struggle, uncertainty, and redirection.

In such scenario we have to shift our Mindset toward positive attitude, because positive attitude doesn't mean ignoring difficulties or pretending everything is perfect, it means choosing to see beyond the immediate challenge and believing in growth, flexibility, and opportunity.

"Progress Over Perfection"

(Progress isn't about perfection, it's about determination)

Perfection is not necessary to be successful but Progress is necessary, have you ever felt like no matter how hard you try, you just aren't where you want to be? Maybe you're working toward a dream, a goal, or even just trying to be better than you were yesterday, we compare ourselves to others who seem to have it all together and think, "What's the point? *I'll never be as good as them,* this mindset can paralyze us. We stop moving forward because we think if we can't do it perfectly, when the road feels long and perfection feels impossible just Keep Showing Up, No Matter What.

you're not supposed to have everything figured out overnight, good things take times, you need to set realistic expectations.

Stop waiting for the "end result" to feel happy, Result is output and activity is inputs, we cannot drive output, Celebrate the journey, the lessons, and the growth that come along the way, Every step counts.

Instead of saying, "I can't do this," try saying, "I can't do this *yet*" That one small word shifts your mindset from defeat to hope.

Progress is in the *quiet persistence*, the small victories, and the faith to keep going, don't let the fear of imperfection hold you back. Don't let the slow pace make you give up. The results will come—just stay the course.

"Strike While the Iron is Hot"

We should not wait for the perfect time but should make the time perfect with our dedication, hard work and a goal.

Waiting for perfection is very dangerous and with this attitude we cannot reach to our Goal.

We are thinking that I will start when I have more time, I will take the leap when I'm more experienced, I will pursue my dreams when everything feels just right, i will take leave for family if everything will be right in office.

If you've had those thoughts, you're not alone. It's natural to want things to feel secure before stepping out. But the truth is, waiting for perfection is like waiting for rain in the desert—it may never happen. Life will always throw challenges our way. There will always be "what-ifs" and fears trying to hold us back.

If still we will wait for perfect time, then definitely, we Lose valuable time that we'll never get back, we Miss opportunities to grow and learn through action and stay stuck in fear, wondering what could have been, the result will be Feel frustrated watching others achieve what we dream about.

Waiting for perfection can feel safe, but it comes at a high cost. The longer we wait, the further away our dreams feel.

You don't need the perfect moment—you just need the courage to take one step forward. That step might be small, but it's a step in the right direction.

Shift Mind Set from "Why" to "How"

What we learn as children shapes us as adults, here we are doing the same thing with asking "Why" Our parents used to ask questions like why this was not done, why you haven't eaten yet and many more "Why" question, when we grow up and apply the same tendencies to our generation, actually this mind set weakens our effectiveness.

For example, if your boss asks to you that I don't think you're quite ready for a promotion then suddenly our reaction will be "Why" not, in that situation instead for reacting through "Why" we should need to understand why boss thinks that you are not ready for promotion, now naturally the situation is you ask why, do you think that I am not ready for promotion, this is Back to front conversations.

The more opportunities you give him to argue against getting the promotion, the harder it will be for him to shift into reverse gear later and admit boss is wrong. "Why?" A conflictual cycle of argument and counter-argument will arise.

In this situation the best conversation should be- I'm obviously disappointed to hear this. I think I deserve for promotion, please let me know how can I provide evidence to demonstrate that I am ready for the promotion, such conversation might be open new door for discussion from new perspective and you can present your achievement and potential for promotion.

My Friends please remember in Life that "why" is always backward-looking and "how" focuses on the future and the Gateway for Solution.

Favouritism- Unspoken reality in the workplace which stealthily diminishing job satisfaction and team morale.

Favouritism is a very big issue in current scenario which we can't imagine, I can understand that many people must have gone through this situation in their professional career.

When you came to know that your boss has a clear favourite, in that situation staying positive and motivated is very tough.

In few studies showing that more than 50% Manager decided promotion and increment to their choicest employee before completing Appraisal Process.

favouritism can be hard to pinpoint and quantify but we with few actions you can navigate this complex and challenging situation and improve your projections.

Manage You Emotions and Don't Take Personally

First we need to understand why boss doing Favouritism, it might be maximizing their self-interest and being more familiar with other person or might be their lacking awareness they are favouring due to their implicit biases.

In such situation you might be dislike your boss, want to vent with your colleagues or confront your boss which we must to avoid these reactions, the best move is we must think that favouritism doesn't exist and seek to encourage a stronger relationship.

Just think and put yourself in place of boss and reflect their Goal and Pressure and think and start working the way you can make their life easier at the same time we observe our colleague that what they are doing well that make them successful with your boss, after all above activity we have to communicate very Proactively with Boss because When you feel like you're not favoured, you may hesitate to proactively communicate with your boss.

Come Out from Concept "Good work speaks for itself"

This concept should be idealistic, but remember my friend idealistic to think your boss will notice all your talents and achievements without you highlighting them then it's wrong thinking, you must make your hard work and accomplishments known.

We must summarize our achievement weekly or in every Milestone and update to boss through email or in writing during your one-on-ones and by highlighting your team's work in meetings.

Nurture your internal network, Enhance Relationship with Cross Functional Team

Emerging a robust network can enhancement your job performance and satisfaction and is vital to your career success. It's even more crucial if you're not receiving guidance, recognition, and opportunities from your boss

After doing all above activity, learning if still your Boss doing Favouritism, then I can say only, If you can't change the Boss, Change the Boss.

"Be the Best Version of Yourself"

first you need to understand that your work reflects you therefore work on yourself, not the job.

self-improvement in key of bringing your best, why you are waiting to others to tell you about how you can improve yourself, here are few actions where we can follow and start day to day improvement for best version of yourself.

Change weaknesses into strengths and take step to rectify career limiting behaviour.

Set Realistic Goal and Track it, setting goals for yourself doesn't just give you a sense of purpose in life but also makes you accountable for your decisions and action, there's no point in setting goals if you don't follow through with it, figure out simple motivational moves to get yourself to implement your plan of action.

Find opportunity to Learn because Learning is way of Life- this should be top priority I your day-to-day activity, you can learn from anyone from your colleague, Boss, Office boy even from inanimate and animate.

You should avoid multitasking because doing multitasking at once can decrease productivity, Tackle one task at a time because you don't lose anything by not multitasking.

Don't overcommit, before you take on additional work, pause and check if you're able to take on that work. Learn to say "no" at work more frequently, delegate the work to your team members if possible.

Deliver result consistently as per plan with a disciplined approach and methods and always accountable for result.

"Basic Mantra of Success"

(Inclination + Commitment + Dedication)

One thing is inclination, do you have inclination towards a particular job, is that why you are thinking in that direction or do you take the decision on the basis of what they will get from it, will I get this kind of salary or may I get this kind of salary? Will be able to earn money or lifestyle of Many people think about this but this is the wrong way, because in this way you will have everything and at the end of life you will have nothing, We have to think very seriously that life is a very precious thing and we should be concerned about what we are going to spend our life on, should you do something because someone else is doing it or should you not do it because of No one else is doing it, you should do it only if it really matters to you.

Dedication - If your heart isn't in something then you won't do your best. If you don't do your best then great things will happen to you, whether it's art, music, design, business, sports or politics, it doesn't matter. what is that If you are not completely dedicated to what you are doing then you will never be able to do any important work in your life, this is absolutely certain, you may earn a living but you will not be able to do anything important.

Let me take an example, you must have heard the name Virat Kohli, this man knows nothing except hitting the ball, his entire dedication is just to hit the ball and keep hitting it, now he is a great player It's just dedication, you try talking to him one on one, you talk about the ball, he is so dedicated to it, it is his religion and sacred thing, it is everything to him, he spends his whole life working for a simple task like the ball. put into killing We should think that if we start our life today, will I be able to remain dedicated to what I am doing now for the next 20 years, will it be important to me, will I feel satisfied if I look back and see that I have what have you done Do whatever you want, just do it well, it's important and don't do anything that you will be embarrassed about tomorrow, it doesn't matter what other people say but you should not be ashamed of your work, Do whatever you want, just do it well, it's important and don't do anything that you will be embarrassed about tomorrow, it doesn't matter what other people say but you should not be ashamed of your work.

You must do this much in your life, if you leave this thing then you will live a very ordinary life. You may have everything but you will have nothing.

"Keep Burning the Midnight Oil"

At night the boundaries become blurred, hence night is more helpful for studies and focus, our eyes are made in a special way, light shows us everything differently, if we are sitting in light, we can see everything around us. We can see only one group in the dark.

This is the reason why boundaries become blurred at night, this is why night is very helpful for studies and focus because at night the difference between each other becomes less.

I concentrate more at night, concentrate more while doing work and also the mind remains more alert in night, Creative energy increases at night. When this happens, the energy flow in the brain is more than during the day, due to this when you try to read and memorize Hindi, English or any such creative subject, it gets memorized very quickly.

For this reason, you should remember at night. There is a fear of falling asleep at night, that is why you should study aloud and instead of memorizing while sitting, you should memorize while walking. The more you memorize, the stronger your brain will become and the faster you will be able to memorize.

"Be Adaptable and Flexible"

Instead of making your personality solid, you should make it flexible, personality is not a matter of anyone being right or wrong, the origin of the word personality is from the Greek word persona which means mask or facade.

We have to wear different types of masks to perform different tasks, for example if you are playing a sport then different types of masks should be worn which should be aggressive which should arouse fear in the opposite team, if we are in the office then different kind of mask But if we are at home, we have to wear a completely different kind of mask, when we are with friends, we have to wear a different kind of mask. The true meaning of oratory is that we have to adapt our personality for different tasks, now you will see that a After the age of about thirty to thirty-five, our personality becomes the same even if it is in office, Be it at home or anywhere else, it is not right for our life in any way, we have to play the role of our personality according to the situation, the thing is that we may wear any kind of mask but we are We remain the same, we do not understand the difference between ourselves and the mask, hence we all should wear the mask consciously.

"The Leadership Mantra"

first time manager needs to learn from day one how to delegate well, proposed few actions where first time manager can start working on this for self-improvement and Learning.

Shift Mindset from doing to managing

First time manager means promoted from previous job where as a individual performance was good and result was as expected by management, but after promotion as First Time Manager here role and responsibility is changed now, you must accept that you cannot do everything on your own.

As a manager success is not only equal to being the best performer on your team but it should be Strong mindset by your ability and experience to help team to grow and reach their goal and contribute to the larger Organization vision, your decision can impact their career trajectory.

Listen to your Team

As a new Manager might be feel pressure to come up with the answer, we must listen to team member, skilful listening is very important because this will support to understand the fact and implication of any action, Open- ended question led to better more clear answer that closed Yes or No question, at the same time we have to consider a range of option and alternatives.

"Empower Your Team"

(Are Leaders Doing Team's Work for Them, If Yes Stopped Doing Immediately)

Many leaders and seniors are working one level below which is very dangerous for our Team members and such practices paralyzed and killed learning skill and growth of Team members, we must Stop immediately.

As a Leader when we started Team's work for them rather than Guiding, Motivating and allowing them to grow, NO ONE Wins and the overall capability of Team members continue weak and Organization thinking might be that Leaders not able to capable and hold them to standard and Leaders likely become trapped in a spiral of high workload.

Please remember Every minute you spend doing someone else's job is a minute you spend not doing your own.

Build Capability Below Leaders

When any Team member is not able to deliver expected results then as a Leader our job should be Support, encourage and motivate them to do their job at the same time we must ensure that team.

Aware about our process, policy, mission and vision and having sufficient tools and Training for improvement of performance.

Work Approach Should Be Like a Coach Instead Team Caption

For a Leader working and thinking approach should be like Coach Instead Captain, because captain striving to be best player on the filed but as a Coach job is different, Coach observes the Game, plan a winning strategy and given Guidance, Direction and motivating to Team to play at their peak.

Think About Future

As a Leader our Goal should not be make ourself essential for our Team, it should be made ourself redundant build a Team that can function without us.

We have to keep in mind that putting performance pressure on our team is not harsh but it's purely selfless act by any Leader, that's why our mindset should be to focus on getting the best outcomes you possibly can with the resources that our organization has trusted on us.

"Be Human First, Employee Second"

(The Way of Transforming Potential to Performance)

It is important to know our employees before we can understand our business, Employee, Customer all are human therefore we lead all our stakeholder by humanity only, please don't just consider as worker to your employees, that they are individuals with personal lives, emotions, and needs, and should be treated with respect and consideration as such, prioritizing their well-being and overall humanity within the workplace.

This method recognizes that employees are not just resources to be managed but rather individuals with unique needs, aspirations, and capabilities.

We have to create an empathetic environment that allows coworkers to be transparent.

we have to encouraging people to open up a little bit, so employees can talk without fear and managers can listen without judgement.

The cycle of success for our Business are

Employee Selection is Key of any successful business, we must care about selection that we have to select for Attitude and Train for Skills because Skills can be taught, but it's difficult to train someone to have the right attitude. The most successful service organizations hire first for attitude and only secondly for skills. They train new hires in the skills they need for their jobs.

After selection make sure that new employees receive training in the skills and tools they need to perform their jobs well. Training should include an appropriate mix of interpersonal and technical skills.

After Completing Training, we have to give an opportunity to WIN on their job and we must provide tools and support they need therefore they will perform better and feel better about their jobs, my experience is Without adequate support systems, even the best employee cannot provide the results and service that they want to give customers. Well-designed support systems, such as technology, information systems, workplace design, and service facilities, all contribute to employee capability.

We have to allow freedom within Limit because, Micromanagement is disparaging and frustrating to capable employees. They resent being treated as incompetent, and they become dissatisfied with their work. Their productivity declines. The most valuable employees will find work somewhere else.

Recognize and reward your people for their continuing contributions to service. Rewards should reflect the culture and values of organization and should take into account what motivates your employees.

"Develop Your People Skills"

Important aspects of starting a job is adopt new Culture of Organization, navigate the social dynamics of your workplace, understand departmental and Organization priorities.

Understanding of own role in the context of larger organizational goal.

At the same time its most important that how to build a good relationship with colleagues and specially with Boss, because your boss will play the most influence roll in your professional life, Boss can facilitate lots of things, information and can your integration within Team and organization, being proactive in building a good relationship with your boss can be extremely beneficial to your career, as most managers judge proactive newcomers more favorably in both the short and long term.

Image your upcoming personality- The first step is to imagine what you want your relationship with your boss to look like. Having a clear image of the type of relationship you want to build will help you identify the actions and behaviours you need to accept to make it happen.

Make an Action Plan- When you have acknowledged the type of relationship you want to have, think about how you will make your vision a reality. Start by making an action plan and Always Believe in your power and regular monitor your relationship index.

Admiration diverse sentiments and attempt to understand viewpoints of individuals.

Must focus on self-development and consistently learn from others in team.

Demonstrate commitment and going beyond the call of duty if required.

Display enthusiasm and hopefulness about work.

Understanding and enjoy working with cross functional team.

"How to Make Great Decisions, Quickly"

Once in the jungle a lion falls into a big pit, The monkey was hanging on a tree next to the pit Seeing the lion falling into the pit, the monkey started making fun of him, and started saying that become a bigger lion, now hunters will come and take away your skin, will tear your eyes out, will take away all your arrogance, oh yes, we will have a lot of fun watching all this, you used to trouble many animals, now you will be troubled, While the monkey was saying all this, the branch on which he was sitting broken and the monkey came to one side and fell into the same pit in which the lion had fallen As soon as the monkey fell into the pit, he said, Mother swear, that I have fallen from the tree just to ask for your forgiveness.

From this Story we can Learn from Monkey that we can take good decision without hesitation and postponement to address root cause not only symptoms.

"Streamline Your Path"

happiness = no obligation.

Happiness + No Obligations = Moments of Clarity.

Moments of clarity = ability to make decisions and stand firm.

Ability to take decisions and remain firm = path to reach goal.

When you choose a destination for yourself or a goal for yourself, then decision making becomes a very important part to reach that goal, and we are able to take appropriate decisions only when we are at the moment of clarity and when we take a decision clearly, we should stick to our decision no matter what, Because when we are under some compulsion and are not clear and many types of thoughts keep coming in our mind then we will not stick to a decision and if we do not stick to our decision and keep changing our direction then we will get lost endlessly and will not be interested in doing anything.

What is important, Time Management or Energy Management

Life is alive with two things; one is time and the other is energy. We cannot manage time because whether we are sleeping, awake or doing anything or not, time keeps passing, Time does not move slowly or fast for anyone, it moves at the same speed for everyone, we can neither reduce nor increase the speed of time in any way nor can we stop it, hence there is no such thing as time management. Things don't happen because we have no control over them, we can only manage energy, if we keep our energy level high then we can do any work in less time which would take more time for other people to do, this means we can improve our life. can live more happily, If life remains energetic and more joyful then there will be an increase in life because we cannot increase time but we can increase life by increasing our energy.

We must master time to determine the nature of our destiny, and the only way to master time is to master the way our energies work, If we work like an old steam engine, it will take a lot of time and if we work like a jet engine, it will take a lot of time, yes there is no mastery over time but the result is mastery over time, a special mobilization of life time and energy. we have to understand its nature.

Energy management is an important skill in today's world as many people suffer from burnout these days. While increasing productivity at any task requires actually focusing, feeling motivated, and staying healthy, energy can be managed in a number of ways.

Physical Energy – This energy is completely related to health which is influenced by sleep routine, calorie intake and exercise. By following a nutritious diet and taking timely diet and necessary activities, we can ensure that we have all the required energy. Energy required to perform tasks efficiently.

Emotional Energy- This is an important part of energy management, if we are in positive emotional state then we can conserve our energy and if we are in negative emotional state then we destroy our energy very quickly and easily, to increase emotional energy, we should celebrate small victories and stop blaming ourselves for every small mistake.

Spiritual Energy- To understand this energy well, first of all we have to understand the purpose of our work, this type of energy is deeply related to the faith and belief of the person.

Mental Energy- To increase this energy, it is necessary to have a clear and concentrated mind, this energy can be best utilized through meditation.

Social Energy- It helps in energizing the social life of a person. Whether you're an extrovert, an introvert, or an ambivert, social interactions can have an incredible impact on your energy, Lack of social interaction can have a negative impact on your energy, causing your productivity levels to decline. You can improve your social energy by interacting with friends and relatives and going out for walks.

"The Right Approach to Handle a Team"

"Your team believes that you don't trust them with their work, they'll struggle to trust you with their growth and learning"

As a manager this is very important to establishing Trust within your team, your direct reports must have confidence in your ability to make decision, communicate effectively and help them grow in order to perform to the best of their abilities.

All above things also depending how you arrive in your new role, promoted from within team or hired from other Organization or other department from within organization.

When you lead such a team member, you have worked with them before then, it's easy to want to hold them to the standard you performed at. Your ability to do this work well is likely how you distinguished yourself and got your promotion but at the same time there are few fears that if your direct reports aren't able to do the work as well as you did, it will reflect poorly on your leadership.

Make an effort to help your direct reports master their tasks in their own way. Measure their abilities against yours when you started doing the work — when you were first learning. Use your expertise judiciously, avoiding comparisons or being overly corrective. You can say something like, tell me how I can best use my experience in this work to help you grow.

At the same time, you have to clear expectations around deliverables, KPIs, and deadlines. Agree on the outcomes you both believe they can achieve, and the approach they feel most comfortable taking, Then, let them figure out how to achieve the goals you set, leveraging your guidance when they need it.

The hard truth is that once you become a leader, the relational boundaries with your former peers must shift. Similarly, if you were hired from the outside, you must set appropriate boundaries with your new team members. Your ability to socialize with them, what information you share with them, and what information they share with you, must be carefully thought through, if you were promoted from within the company, having a proactive conversation with each person with whom your relationship has changed will enable you to clarify what they can expect from you as their leader.

build confidence by looking confident

You must stability confidence with humility, authenticity, and vulnerability so that the trust you earn is well-rounded and grounded in your full humanity. In the face of uncertainties, budget shortfalls, your team needs to know you are comfortable not having all the answers.

Building trustworthiness through past achievements

As a new leader, it's important to build trustworthiness. You may be attracted to rely on your track-record of positive results to make people trust your decision-making and leadership abilities.

Building and maintaining trust with your team is a long process. While you may be anxious about performing well in your new role, it's important not to rush things. Listen to your feelings of anxiety and self-doubt, but don't let them weaken trust on your team. Stay focused on your larger goal of genuinely earning trust over time with your full humanity, experience, and desire to make your direct reports as successful as they can be.

"Be a Jack of All Trades"

My request and advice to your professional is Don't Just Focus on Your Technical Skills. Focus On Your People Skills, though technical skills may help you to achieve your first promotions, they won't help you as much three or four years down the line. As we advance to more senior roles, a greater emphasis and value is placed on interpersonal skills, People skills to help you how work on your own and with others.

To be a real leader, you must first understand how to be effective in that follower role. One way to do this is to manage up, down, and sideways. To achieve any long-term goal, you will eventually need your bosses to supporter for you, and your peers to authenticate your ideas, and those more junior to you to help you execute.

How to Manage MPS (Manager, Peer, Subordinate) in Corporate Sphere

In day-to-day corporate life, we often have to create better coordination with three people so that the business function runs smoothly.

Manage Up- Managers

First of all, we all respect to our manager and their time and Goal, we have to clear a big picture in mind and must understand how to our daily activity fit into in this picture, if both are aligned and in one page then definitely reach goals quickly.

Any time you approach your manager with an idea, make sure that you understand the strategic issues they're facing. Ask yourself: What problems are stopping them from reaching their long-term goals? What can I do in my role to help them overcome these challenges.

Might be Your solutions don't have to be "right," but having a clear and evidence-backed perspective will demonstrate your problem-solving abilities.

Manage Up- Peers

Peers' role is very important in our day-to-day activity and support, we must build strong bounding and need to create such environment where we able to share feedback which we need to implements new idea and process.

This will permit you to gain valuable insights, course correct, and create a more realistic plan of action. Knowledge sharing also has the potential to energize and inspire both you and your teammates.

Manage Up- Subordinate

Handholding, Mentoring and Teaching is very important to our Subordinate, these are a Great way to improve Leadership skills as well you can gain support from people who understand how you think and who can help you execute the task with more efficiently and effectively.

"The Way to Be Super Productive"

Being productive is not about doing more but about doing things in an efficient manner.

Time is not under our control and we can't it, we are sleeping, we are awake, time is running out, we are doing anything but time is running out but Energy we can Manage through various activity and discipline and that energy will save time and enhance capacity to complete task within timeframe.

Consider creating rules around your own schedule. If you are most alert in the mornings, try to schedule your most demanding tasks and meetings early.

Check your email 3-4 Times in a day therefore focused on another task without distraction

You should avoid using Mouse during working on system because few research showing That 3 seconds per minute of work by using their mouse instead of keyboard shortcuts, learning keyboard shortcuts can be massive for productivity.

reflect what habits you want to change and think about how you can alter your environment to influence those behaviours.

"The Power of Small Step"

It's great to dream big, but the way to achieve big is to start small

Micro habits help you to complete big goals, in many times We are educated and rewarded to think big, not to do small things, we may feel silly while doing something small and we avoid doing them, the benefit of micro habits is that you should be able to perform it with minimal effort every day, after starting small task we must measure this, What gets measured, gets done, Start and hold steady for a long time.

"Treat Your Career Like a Portfolio"

First, we have to understand what is Career Portfolio, it's not like investment portfolio, Diversified fund portfolio, it's not like term of Finance or Business, it's not a physical or system entity but its new way to think, talk about, but it's a set of skills which is very important in Professional life which work with purpose clarity and flexibility.

Career path work like in one direction with focused on what is traditional ahead and career portfolio is a never-ending source of finding and fulfilment.

Today the world is changing in amazing and deep way Expansion your career focus and professional identity is no longer seen as irregular.

A portfolio allows you to make creative connections between your skills and apply them to a variety of opportunities.

A portfolio can help you stay relevant and build skills and experience.

A portfolio can offer more freedom and engagement, and you don't feel pressured to stick to one role.

Employees who commit to building a career portfolio template are more flexible, more widely skilled, and better equipped to take on future challenges.

Creating Career portfolio is very important for those who has recently join any Organization or just started their Career because Career portfolio gives you more space and wisdom to test out different things and find your way with traditional paid jobs you should think about to create Career Portfolio, don't limit yourself, think bigger, career portfolio will not create by someone it will create by you only.

Its unique combination of skills experience and talent, it directly reflects professional identity and potential.

Someone else gives you the job and determines its scope whether you will move forward or not, on the other side A career portfolio generally leads to greater ownership of your career.

Over a period of time, the value of your portfolio will increase by your ability to cross-pollinate.

The future of work is full of uncertainty. It is hard to know what to do or to trust that things will work out. For all the things that you can't control in today's world, taking ownership of your portfolio is one that you can. You can start today. Your future will thank you.

"Be Visible and Vocal"

"Keep making your identity in silence, your name will hum in the wind itself"

in corporate world this is very important that you noticed by Senior Management especially by your Boss's Boss without bypass to your reporting Boss.

we have often seen that employee having good knowledge, ideas, insights and ambition to take more but employee is not able to express the same to senior management due to your boss is not supportive.

there is No short path to getting noticed, but if you focused on below Key areas with complete dedication, patience with acceptance that this will take some time then you'll keep moving in the right direction and be ready for what's next when it comes.

Always keep in mind Organization's Value and Purpose because the Value and Purpose reflecting what is and isn't expected of employees.

Raise your hand. Don't be afraid to ask for opportunities to show your skills and talents, if you believe that in any specific area you can contribute better which will be benefit for Organization then Freely ask for participate and explain why you believe you can make a valuable contribution.

Demonstrate your commitment to your growth and to the Organization, this is One way to show how serious you are and you are ready to take any challenges and opportunity.

Focus on team success rather than your own, leadership notices those who work collaboratively and support others, envisioning the future with respect to area of work by keeping larger picture in mind.

Know your number, take ownership and honour your value of Commitment.

Challenge old ways and find new solutions, discover new practices which are better than existing best practices, see a different approach to a problem your company is facing, see a different approach and method of working, the more you work on it, the better you'll get.

Build strong relationship with other team members, cross functional team members, look for opportunities to connect and collaborate with other key players in your organization therefore you Can increase your visibility and influence, Great leaders don't just wait to be asked, they put themselves in positions and situations where they're more likely to be asked.

You don't have to be clever but you have to be thoughtful remember it.

"How to Beat a Checkmate"

Somewhere many employees face the such situation in their corporate career, this is not a Normal situation, it's very difficult to deal with a boss who is shutting you out, you can visualize that your boss is very supportive and provide you open opportunity in career growth in an ideal world, but unfortunately the world is not ideal.

If your boss decided to shutting you out then he can stop answering to you, can exclude in important meeting or task and many more particularly if they know you disagree with them.

Here are few activities, action plan where you can follow up for damage control or for repair the relationship with your Boss.

Analyze the situation & revisit your assumptions

First of all, you have to analyze the situation that how your boss treating you compare to others team members.

Follow RRR Concept (Reengineering, Repair, Relationship)

Show your boss that you valued them and want and working to improve relationship, request help from your boss for way forward.

Put your performance at High level

Such relationship can't be repair immediately, focus on your performance and put it high because as long as there is performance, you are there, otherwise, you can give one more reason for shutting you out because few Boss are waiting, Such situation to out you immediately.

"Right Approach of Performance Discussion"

"We should think that Employees are not Sheep and Manager are not shepherd who will get the work done with a stick every day"

in current scenario many employees are facing mentally torcher by their manager due to unprofessional discussion.

managers are starting discussion with shouting and very rough language and spoken that i don't know anything but you have to do it, few managers are only mission to finding fault in employee in every discussion, there is No any sense how to engage an employee to their commitment toward Organization Here are few Stop for healthy discussion during performance review or day to day review.

Follow the concept of GEM – Groundwork Empathy Motivation

Before discussion with an employee, I think you should work on what is Ground reality, current market and industry scenario, possibility to stretch and then you have to start discussion with an employee with Empathy not start from shouting and rough language, this will create a Positive and healthy discussion platform and employee will engage and learn from discussion otherwise You keep abusing on the call and the employee will keep abusing you by turning aside the phone but in his mind because he can't keep on shouting like you to take care of his job and family.

When we start working with knowing ground reality and with empathy then employee will self-motivated to take any challenges to deliver their best because this is not work for a day or week or month.

Set a Platform for Collaboration with Manager and Employee

Request to all Manager come out from Fault Finding Mission and work collaboratively to define a shared commitment to growth and development.

This is very important to create a platform where employee can feel free to share actual things of ground level with honest therefore employee feel himself valued and supported.

At the same time manager should understand employees' value sense of engagement and commitment to organization.

Manager must aware to every employee that how their current action and performance connect to their long-term career path.

Manager should provide clear example instead hypotheticals and we should avoid ambiguity During review or feedback.

Focus Shift from Blame Game to wards collaborative problem-solving and growth

We have to understand and accept that management is not at fault., 3 Problem are always remained with State level and below, Leadership Communication and Relationship.

Sometimes we have also seen that if a senior management created wrong policy and he aware about it after so many feedback given by local team based on industry trend and market requirement then instead of correcting the policy with Senior management, all the blame falls on the employee that employee are not able to handle State or location and also not able to understand the policy, This is very danger situation for an Employee and Organization as well, I Called to such Boss – The Accidental Boss who haven't known about Industry, Business Trend even not able to listen of any employee regarding this.

With such Accidental Boss Employee suffering from mentally pain and Organization suffering from low Productivity and Brand reputation.

Management must identify such Accidental Boss and should take corrective action to save Organization Value.

It's also critical that you leave judgment aside and approach the discussion as an inquiry, acknowledging the emotional aspect of the conversation.

Ask your employee to share their honest opinion about what is leading to this feedback, then sit in silence and give them space to share their thoughts.

After above discussion with employee, we must provide an Actionable Path considering focus on right approach of work and future growth.

Help the team become aware of risk and opportunity of different factors contributing to sustainable business.

Support to team through the change process and helps individuals deal with ambiguity.

Take end to end ownership of Goal instead blame to down the line team.

Remember TTC- Trust Team work and Collaboration is only Mantra of Success.

Offer a non-threatening environment to bring people together for Common Goal and Purpose.

"The Right Approach to Get Promotion"

A promotion is an exciting thing, you assume more responsibilities, step up to the next role

apart from job well done, actually getting promotion takes more, even you are high performer and you achieved surpassed expectation, you often still have to convince your manager that you deserve for next level, promotion doesn't happen overnight, there are a few ways to go about this.

apart from your day-to-day activity and during annual performance review you should focus on what will be required for next level of career.

you talk about possibility of promotion in future with your manager during your one-to-one discussion, The Right time for discussion the same is achieve a major goal and lets other team members and cross functional team appraise for your work then start promotion possibility discussion with manager.

You required a sponsor within your organization who is in a position of power and will support you for the same; after identifying sponsor you have to meet them on Tea / coffee and enhance your relationship therefore sponsor seek their feedback on your work and advice for how to reach your goal and also advocate for you behind closed doors.

Create a folder and document all your achievements therefore you can use these as evidence to support your case, instead of self-promote, you have to advocate, there is a thin line between evidence-based advocating versus generic self-promotion.

Create your own clone, apart from above activity you have to create your own clone and create them for next level of career, Management will promote you for next level after verifying that you have create a team member who can take your responsibility to avoid any loss to Organization.

"Dos and Don'ts - If You Know More Than Your Boss"

There are instances where newer professional has more experience in certain areas than Reporting manager, this could be deeper understanding you frow up with newly technology. In such situation you have to take care how leverage your knowledge, skills and experience While maintain humility, balance approached and collaborative mind.

Do's

As digital Natives generation you may have better understanding about digital platform and technological expertise, your approach should be collaboratively, if you're being asked to do something that you know could be done better with a different tool, approach the conversation with curiosity. Start by acknowledging your manager's experience and expertise, and propose the idea in the form of a question to create an open dialogue.

Setting your understandings as resources for the team, this approach frames the information as a proactive idea for team advancement.

Adopt a learning approach.

Add value to joint initiatives when leadership capabilities are needed.

Maintain a respectful and professional attitude.

Be a valuable asset.

Develop a strong rapport with your boss by actively listening and showing genuine interest their perspective.

Don'ts

Do not show as a self-proclaimed expert.

Avoid undermining their authority by publicly disagreeing or gossiping.

If you disagree with a decision, discuss it privately with your boss, explaining your concern Respectfully.

Instead of saying "you're wrong," say "Have you considered this approach.

If you are disagreeing with any topic with Boss, always maintain a professional demeanour and avoid publicly criticizing their decisions, recognize that your boss may have different experiences and priorities.

How to Manage a "Toxic Boss"

in current scenario this is very serious concern, toxic boss should be taken very seriously.

toxic bosses are more susceptible to chronic stress, depression, and anxiety, staying in a job with toxic Boss can be ever dangerous, they trust feedback from third parties more than you.

Difficult boss may not be open to hearing feedback about his or her failings; to prove himself right in front of the management, he can cut the professional throat of any team member. The situation is such that one can neither swallow nor spit, employee suffer from emotional exhaustion.

Toxic boss thinking Aham Brahmasmi (I am God" or "I am the universe) and does not provide Correct information to Management.

Employee Situation in such scenario

Decision of job quitting is very hard because many employees are emotionally attached and engaged in their job.

Things might get better.

I can't afford to take pay cut in other organization.

I have invested so much time here, will start with new in other organization.

I don't want to lose the benefit of Appraisal and Increments.

I don't have a skill to get different job.

How to Manage such situation

Bad bosses should be taken seriously. If quitting is not an immediate option, there are some practical things you can do to mitigate the potential damage of working for a toxic boss.

Put your mode on Request instead Feedback, because toxic boss will never hear your feedback.

In such emotionally challenging situation, you have to active and engage with your supporting network, either your cross functional team, friends, family members who may support and encourage you.

You have to take care your mental and physical health, do some exercise / yoga, take good slip.

Find activities outside of work that bring you joy and satisfaction.

With support of Internal Job Posting process explore other opportunity within Organization.

Consult with team HR, they may have already helped others in the exact same situation.

The situation when you know this time is for quit the job

if you are spending more time about your boss than your work.

if you feel mentally unsafe at work.

if your self -esteem has dropped.

if you think your career progress is stopped here in such scenario.

at above situation you must give your self-permission to quit the job, I am sure thing will better, Line up your next move. There is no magic bullet here you just need start the job search.

The Monkey PIP (Precision Improvement Plan)

The time is to shift from PIP (Performance Improvement Plan to PIP (Precision Improvement Plan).

When there is leakage in the bottle, first attention is paid to the top and not to the bottom. Similarly, if any problem starts in the organization, then we should first pay attention to the senior management and not on the bottom employee.

I hope everyone has heard the name of Pip Performance Improvement Plan, nowadays it is trending in the corporate sector, everyone is racing to give pip to their employee, looks like the manager who gives the most pip will get the best promotion and increment, nowadays people are treating Pip as a weapon of threat, and doing exactly the opposite of Pip's original purpose, On hearing the name of Pip, the heart melts and the employee immediately reaches a state of mental stress, and many managers take advantage of this situation.

We must understand Result, Performance is output and this is not in our control, Inputs, activity and accuracy in our hand which we can improve for better performance.

First of all, we must change the full form of PIP this should be Precision Improvement Plan. Because Result is not in our hand but we can correct our Precision our process our way of working and many Activities which is in our hand which concerted in Performance.

i tell you all a story-

We all know that the king of the jungle is the lion, The lion keeps troubling some animal every day and eats some animal on regular basis, All the animals in the forest were very upset.

One day all animal met together and decided that why don't we change the king of the jungle? Because we all are very upset with the lion, Everyone supported this proposal, But there was no final decision on who should be made king, After much discussion, if it was decided that the monkey is the most agile and intelligent person then why don't we make the monkey the king, After much discussion it was finalized that Monkey should be made the king, and everyone declared the monkey the king and started cheering, The lion came to know that the monkey has been made the king of the jungle, The lion came to the forest very angry and started roaring loudly, Shane said, you all have made the monkey the king, you all will be punished for this, And I will eat this goat tomorrow and if your king has the courage, he will save it, Next day the lion came and started eating the goat, seeing this all the animals in the jungle started shouting loudly that monkey king, save the goat, you are the king of the jungle, Hearing this, the monkey climbed a tree and kept jumping from one tree to another and the monkey regularly jumped from one tree to another, After some time the lion ate the goat and went away, Now the monkey came down from the tree, all the animals told the monkey that we had made you our king and you could not save the goat, Monkey was completely tired and drenched in sweat, And he said, you all have made me your king, I also tried my best, I kept running from one tree to another, but did not rest even for a moment, I kept running continuously.

The monkey in this story is an employee who worked hard to fulfill his responsibilities but kept running but did not get results because he had to save the goat and he could not do it.

Seeing the monkey's efforts Now you have to decide whether you will give Pip to Monkey or Monkey's manager.

I strongly recommended to all Corporate Management, Request Change PIP Meaning first this should be **Precision Improvement Plan** Instead Performance Improvement Plan.

our Field Team working very Hard and we all ware their sacrifices during job, Request before issuing PIP to any filed Employee, please crate a process to issue Monkey PIP to Reporting Manager to just Review and Preparation for below Points, in this PIP we should know from Reporting Manager in written that.

Have Reporting Manager given proper Handholding and Training after joining employee.

Have Manager aware about employees Job Role / KRA Properly.

Have Manager aware about Process / Policy to Employee.

Have proper allocation of Industry and Business Potential aligned with Employee.

Have Manager Provide Tools and Support to Employee based on Market and Industry trend to compete in Market with other competitors.

Have Manager added their Value at time of initial stage of poor performance by employee.

Manager Having Backup Plan and any Alternate to address Employee Low Performance before PIP.

I've seen managers put employees on a PIP before ever addressing the above issues with the employee first! PIPs are often an extreme measure, which means the manager is waiting too long to address the issues or the employee is taking too long to address the issues, in these cases, HR should ask managers, "What conversations have you had with the employee regarding their performance on initial stage.

Request to all Employee who get a PIP follow DND Rules (Discuss, Negotiate, Don't Sign It)-

A good PIP is well documented and detailed. So, when you are reviewing it, talk with your manager with any areas with which you disagree. Take your time and address any and everything that feels out of line. Don't be defensive. Just state the facts.

Make sure the expectations and time for completion are sensible and realistic. If it's not, then ask for an extension, additional help, resources, or anything you feel would level the playing ground and promote your success.

If you don't agree with what's in the PIP and your manager isn't willing to negotiate or discuss...don't sign it. To be clear, this still means you should be looking but don't sign it and don't give in to any pressure.

"The Way to Address Mid-Career Crisis"

Some things are very worrying for a mid-career employee Am I in the right company and right job because mid-career employee who may be searching for execution while manipulating demands at home and penetrating financial pressures to earn, such period are very crucial for any employee, in such scenario few organization taking inhumanity action by issuing PIP, Under Productive Rating and forcefully resignation of employees who working from last 10-15 years with same Organization and due to some internal and external circumstances current performance is not up to the mark.

Midlife is the time where you lose the impression of immortality. You know your opportunities aren't endless, and you understand that time is limited, even people who have achieved a great deal of career success aren't immune to these feelings.

A "midlife career change" refers to making a significant shift in one's professional path later in life, typically during the mid-career stage, often driven by a desire for greater fulfilment, a change in personal priorities, or a need to adapt to evolving market demands; it involves identifying transferable skills from one field to another and potentially pursuing further education or training to enter a new career path.

My friends we must learn and find out right solution of these situation.

Replicate and reframe

When you have a sense of sickness, you start to question everything but you need to break down the problem and start with the place where it hurts, I know this is not easy to rethink professional path in this age where lots of responsibility having of professional and personal.

Do Small Changes and Improvement

if you cannot change your circumstances, you might be able to change the microenvironment in which you operate, for example you can request for transfer in another department or in Committee or for another project.

rejuvenating your commitments" can have a big impact on your viewpoint and viewpoint.

Learning is the way of Life, Focus on Learning

One of the biggest culprits of middle-age career sickness is boredom, when you hit your forties, "you know what you're doing and you're good at it, so you get bored this time you have to consider cross move, ask yourself-Is up the only way?' Perhaps you don't have to hike the ranking if you can do something interesting that will allow you to learn and grow.

Challenge your expectations

Your spirits of professional sickness could also be a sign that your job looms too large. Perhaps "you are being choked by a culture that wants to keep you in a state of being continually obsessed with your career.

Self-assessment

Investigative existing skills and experience to identify transferable abilities that can be applied in a new field, acquiring necessary skills through courses, certifications, or further education to qualify for the desired career.

Networking

Building connections within the new industry to access opportunities and gain insights.

Next Move Might be Helpful

Assessing potential income changes and making necessary adjustments to your budget Overcoming fears and embracing the opportunity for personal growth.

Seeking guidance from mentors, career counsellors, or peers who have transitioned careers.

"Preventing Burnout"

Burnout is the fatigue caused by excessive workload in the office or due to work pressure, due to which people feel unfulfilled and tired and think of leaving the job. What are the main causes of burnout and how to avoid it? We will discuss this further.

Workload - If the workload matches the capacity of the employee, then the employee can do the work properly and at the same time he can balance between his work and other aspects of life and can work to improve himself, To remove the stress of our workload, first of all we have to evaluate ourselves how well we are doing in our field, what planning we are doing for our workload, whether we are giving priority to our work, whether we are managing our time. and proper adjustment of energy.

Feeling a lack of control – Are we feeling like we do not have autonomy and are not able to make important decisions about our professional lives or have a say in all these things, Because of which we are not able to move forward and if we feel like this then immediately step back and ask yourself what could be the reason for such a situation.

For example, does your boss talk to you day and night regarding work and can you ask to be contacted at any time? Do work priorities keep changing in your office, keeping all these aspects in mind, we should assess ourselves and ask ourselves how to change this situation, can we tell while talking to our boss that it is not possible to respond 24/7 and we are in a balance situation? come over.

Community

In the workplace, it is very important what kind of people we work with, what kind of environment we work in and how cooperative and trustworthy our relationship is, we cannot choose our associates and our customers but we can choose our Can improve mobility and make things easier.

Impartiality

Do we believe that we get fair and equitable treatment in our workplace, are our contributions appreciated, are we doing better work than you and others and someone else is getting the reward and are we aware of this lack of fairness because you are stressed

In this situation, you should talk to your senior officers with full confidence and if needed, you can request for their suggestions and support.

The organization's values don't match your values.

It is necessary to match our values with the values of the organization, if we do such thing which is necessary for the organization or if it is not matching with the values of the organization then our motivation to persevere and work hard is reduced to a great extent. may be less.

"Achieving Equilibrium"

finding balance doesn't mean splitting your time equally among everything. It's about focusing your energy where it truly counts.

Dividing our time equally across every area in Personal and professional thing is not possible because we having limited time and all priority is not equal.

Giving too much time to one area (like work) at the expense of others (like rest or relationships) drains our energy and leaves us feeling out of control.

The solution for Finding balance in life is we have to shift from equal time concept to planned energy.

Focus on Quality, Not Quantity -Balance isn't about the number of hours you spend on something; it's about the quality of your attention. When you're with your loved ones, be present. When you're working, give it your best effort and always remember the goal isn't perfection, it's progress.

I am sure when you start focusing your energy on what matters most, something beautiful happens like you will start living with purpose and definitely you will feel more at peace and your relationship will grow stronger the same time you will feel more energized and less exhausted.

Be Kind to Yourself -the most effective ways to alleviate stress, worry, and general anxieties about our life is to practice more thoughtful kindness and self-compassion.

"Artificial Pressure is only Cause of Stress"

Natural Pressure- is good thing and its logical, it can help to employee stay motivated and focused to achieve their Goal.

Artificial Pressure- is only Cause of Stress and Stress can have a number of physical and mental health effects, including headaches, muscle tension, anxiety, and depression.

Friends in Corporate sector or in any Sector Employee are very stressed and facing lots of medical problem due to only Artificial Pressure by their Employer.

All organizations talk about mental health and spend a lot of money on various types of awareness and training but the result is negligible.

If we really want to reduce or prevent mental stress, we have to look within ourselves.

Are employees working in accordance with the organization's code of conduct values?

Are we creating artificial pressure on our employees instead of natural pressure?

Are we not giving step-motherly treatment to a particular employee?

Is there factionalism going on in the organization in which employees of one's own group are being made to join the organization?

Let us understand in detail about natural pressure and artificial pressure.

Natural Pressure

workload can help to develop new skills and abilities.

Emotionally connected with Seniors and Organization.

Logical Pressure and Employee can feel and accept it.

Natural Pressure Having ability to transforming potential to Performance.

We learn to respect each other's view and opinion.

Building Trust Team work and Collaboration.

Developing sense of ownership and create trustworthy Culture within Organization.

It willing to learn from mistake.

Artificial Pressure

The accidental boss (The one who got the position by grace) only create Artificial pressure.

To show off to Management and justified their job only.

Such a boss creates his own group in the organization and puts pressure on the employees of another group so that he resigns and they can get the employees of our group to join.

Sometimes they create such pressure in order to show their dominance to other verticals.

It can come in many forms, from tight deadlines and demanding workloads to unrealistic expectations and a cutthroat competitive environment.

Its cause of Stress, Burnout, Exhaustion, Mental Health Problem, Anxiety and Depression Employee are using rough language, shouting on Team.

KCC (Killer Conference Call) before and after working hours which created lots of mentally pressure on Employee in front of Employees Family and Kids, in this situation employee facing lots of Pain and never express it to Family and its badly impacted on employee's personal life as well which we cannot image, with such unethical and unprofessional Artificial pressure what will be Organization Value in Family and Society.

Artificial Pressure working like Cannibal who keeps eating his own employees and Organization values.

My humble request to all Management, Please STOP KCC on immediate basis to protect Organization Value and Employees Personal Loss.

"Who Am I"

Your entire idea of yourself should never be based around your career, because if you judge your job too badly then hating your job feels like hating yourself which is very dangerous.

The work culture in many high-pressure fields frequently rewards working longer hours with raises, prestige, and promotions.

When career success is seen as the ultimate life goal, individuals may feel isolated from their family and peers and this is the reason of Stress as well.

high pressure jobs are paired with a big wage check, persons can find themselves launched into a new socioeconomic class and Our identity is highly influenced by how we present ourselves to others.

Age discrimination can make it particularly difficult for those in the mid to late stages of their career to find a suitable role in their field after a layoff. No matter how it happens, becoming disconnected from a career that procedures the foundation of your identity can lead to bigger issues, such as depression, anxiety, substance use, and aloneness.

To what extent has your job influenced your identity, we can know in a certain way.

Do you keep thinking about your work even outside the office?

Whenever you meet someone, how do you introduce yourself and how much do you talk about the company in this conversation?

How would you feel if you did not have a job?

Please do not let your work weigh you down so much that you lose your identity, by keeping a few small things in mind you can free yourself from this problem.

Do not try to do all the work at the workplace, delegate the work.

You may have some hobbies before starting a job, you can start them little by little like writing a book, playing some sports and many other things.

Restructure your network. Reach out to friends and family to refresh your social circles.

Look beyond your job designation. Reflect reframing your relationship to your career not simply in terms of your company or title, but in terms of your skills that could be used across different backgrounds.

While identifying closely with your career isn't necessarily bad, it makes you vulnerable to a painful identity crisis if you burn out, get laid off, or retire.

"Family Always Matter"

(Children need to develop physically, not digitally)

Our work greatly impacts the lives of our children, especially when both parents are working

With the advent of economic needs and crisis in the society, the family-style has changed in a certain way, where both the parents are engaged at work. Thus, this parent-child relationship has faced huge impacts, both positive and negative.

The growing need of the society, where couples move out of their families to pursue careers and find jobs, has given rise to the nuclear family style, where child care and support from the joint family system is now blurred, although money can buy many things, it cannot buy love and warmth for a growing child. In such a situation, parents can give the love of grandparents to their child.

You must have seen that whenever an employee considers his work, his career above his immediate family and gives importance to him, the thought comes that he has money to feed and mouth to eat.

Such unhappy and stressed employees are teaching their children that money is above everything else, my friends Children consider their parents as ideals. Young minds are like sponges that absorb everything.

The psychological or emotional absence of a father has a deep impact on children. This lack of participation directly affects the child's behavior.

The career choices we make impact our families. Now, because both parents are at work, children are either in school or in the care of baby sitters.

You must have often seen that in today's digital age, people often do their work from home after coming from office, but believe me, when they do so, we can harm our children.

There are some important ways by which parents can balance office and home life and also take care of their children properly.

One should prepare some food at home and all the family members should sit together and eat it together.

While eating, the TV should be switched off and the mobile phone should be kept away.

One should not talk about work while eating with children.

Parents should take out enough time to talk to children.

Family day should be planned once or twice a month and fun activities or sports should be played with children.

"Parachuter vs Gross Router"

First, we have to know about Inclusive Leaders which is very good for Organization and Teams.

At the same time Accidental Boss is very dangerous for Organization and Teams.

Here are few differences where we can clear about both Leadership Style.

Inclusive Leadership

Inclusive Leadership assures that all Team members feel they are treated respectfully and fairly, are valued and sense that they belong, and are confident and inspired.

It does not mean just nice to have on Team but its Impact are very high and enhance employee productivity.

Inclusive Leaders are known for Visible Commitment, They fluent reliable commitment to diversity.

Self-effacement- They are shy about capabilities, admit mistakes, and create the space for others to contribute.

Awareness of bias- They show awareness of personal blind spots as well as faults in the system and work hard to ensure meritocracy.

Curiosity about others- They validate an open mindset and deep curiosity about others, listen without judgment, and seek with empathy to understand those around them.

Effective collaboration- They empower others, pay attention to diversity of thinking and psychological safety, and focus on team cohesion.

Build a Culture of Accountability – Inclusive Leaders are working to Build a culture of accountability where people feel self-motivated and go out of their way to achieve result without compromising on the process.

Build a Culture of Boundary less- inclusive Leaders are build a culture of Boundary less and seamless working where teams generate ideas in an open and supporting environment.

Adding Value to all Stakeholders- Inclusive Leaders are very well known about specified and unspecified needs of multiple Customer segments which support in Leads the process of seeking, capturing and deploying Customer insight.

From Ego Drive to Co- Drive- inclusive Leaders are drive sustainable Business with Co- Drive instead Ego- Drive.

Accidental Leaders

An accidental Leaders are someone who ends up in a leadership role without formal training or a plan to become a leader.

They become Leadership Role by Luck or by support of any GANG or Group.

An Accidental Leaders are communicated wrong ground level information to Management.

An accidental Leaders don't believe on Let's Go; they believe only on GO.

An accidental Leaders are driving Team with Ego- Drive concept which badly impacted on Business and Results are decreased productivity, low morale, high employee turnover, missed opportunities, damaged team dynamics.

Reduced Efficiency

Ineffective decision-making, unclear direction, and micromanagement from accidental leaders can lead to missed deadlines and subpar results, hindering productivity.

Low Morale

Team members can feel undervalued and disengaged when their leader lacks the necessary skills to motivate and support them.

High Employee Resignation- Hired and Fired Concept

Persistent dissatisfaction with leadership can push talented employees to seek opportunities elsewhere, resulting in significant loss of institutional knowledge and expertise.

Poor Team Dynamics

Without strong leadership to guide and facilitate collaboration, teams can become dysfunctional, experiencing conflict and a lack of cohesion.

Missed Opportunities

Incapability to recognize and capitalize on new market trends or strategic initiatives due to a lack of vision and leadership capabilities in Accidental Leaders.

Confusion and Uncertainty

When leaders are unsure of their role or lack a clear vision, it can create confusion among team members, leading to delays and indecision.

Accidental Leader has a double character- they will praise the manager brought from their group and will continue to describe him as a performer in the unathletically and manipulated data.

They will ask questions like these to the manager they bring in Tell me when did the battle of Jhansi take place? And they will ask the same questions to other managers tell me the Name all the people who died in the battle of Jhansi whom they do not like because such managers speak the truth up front What's more, it would not be an exaggeration to not ask for the addresses of all those killed along with their pin codes.

According to the accidental leader, all the mistakes are made by the down the line team members and daily they tell the down the line team members that you are not able to do anything, you are a non-performer, a non-performer, a non-performer and one day you will be down. The line team member will gradually begin to accept that he is a true non-performer.

Accidental leaders need a scapegoat every year on whom they can blame themselves and sacrifice them.

They have more faith in manpower transactions (Hire and Fired) than in business transactions.

"How to Disagree with Your Boss"

There are many adventures happening with the employee, one of them is how he disagrees by his boss or senior on some issue or topic, and there is doubt whether it would be appropriate to do so.

For example, your boss proposes a new initiative or new Process and Policy and you think won't work this process or policy based on your local market knowledge and experience the how you can express or disagree for the same, this is very important, how do you decide whether it's worth speaking up? And if you do, what exactly should you say?

It's a natural human reaction to shy away from disagreeing with a superior, our bodies specialize in survival, so we have a natural bias to avoid situations that might harm us

For such situation We immediately think, my Senior will not like me and I am not aligned with organization or I will get fired.

How to handle such situations? I want to share some tips which I have learned from my career.

Be accurate about the risks

Most Employee incline to overplay the risks involved in speaking up. "Our natural bias is to start by imagining all the things that will go horribly wrong.

First prepare the details about the occurrence of Disagree and prepare the logical and data base details of each Disagree point.

And at the same time, we also have to keep in mind that if we do not speak, how can it affect our business?

It is possible that your colleagues are also illiterate but they are not able to speak and are waiting to see who will speak first, you can also discuss the points of interest with your colleagues to see what they think and what are their inputs.

Decide You have to Wait or Express your Opinion on disagree points

If you have understood all the points correctly then discuss it again with your colleague and get their support, People who can contribute experience or information to your thinking.

Discussing the issue in private will make the powerful person feel less threatened instead of in Meeting or with Group, this will provide comfort to senior for rethinking and reevaluate these points.

There is a possibility that if you disagree on such points in the meeting then you will fall within the target of your senior and there is no need to tell you that once you fall within the target then what can happen.

and once you hit the target, all matter will shift from co-drive to ego-drive for few Bosses, and then you will be told that you have problems with leadership, relationship and communication skills and you are not able to manage at local level and all these things will be told to the management because Few Boss Always Right.

You're more likely to be heard if you can connect your disagreement to a higher purpose. contextualizing your statements so that you're seen not as a disagreeable underling then discussion will become more like a chess game than a boxing match.

The smart way to give the powerful person "psychological safety" and control is Request for Permission for disagree on process / policy and say I have reasons to be disrespectful and I can tell you how it won't work.

Just stay Calm because When we feel panicky, we tend to talk louder and faster, when your body language communicates reluctance or anxiety, it undercuts the message

After you've gotten permission, eloquent the other person's point of view. What is the idea, opinion, or proposal that you're disagreeing with and validate original points.

When you move on to expressing your concerns, watch your language carefully, to avoid any "decision words" such as "short-sighted," "silly," or "quick, they have the potential to be misinterpreted or taken personally.

Admit Senior authority because the person in power is probably going to make the final decision, so acknowledge that but remember Don't backtrack on your opinion or give false praise, though, you want to show respect to the person while maintaining your own self-respect.

"The Importance of Beyond Managing Up to the Boss"

Everyone wants to have a good and healthy relationship with their boss, which is very important for your job and your business.

We must go beyond managing our boss for our professional progress, please invest intentionally in leaders up your chain, people outside your core team because When people of influence know you, they can advocate for you and for your career progression.

You need to meet skip level manager and offer so much value to your manager's manager.

If you're new to the company, you could also share your "fresh-eyes" viewpoint. Leaders rarely get this view, and they often appreciate it. When you add value to your skip level, it's good for your career. At minimum, they might think of you when a new opportunity arises. At maximum, they might promote you or give you a raise.

You have also built a good relationship with your manager's peers so don't put all your eggs in your manager's basket. At minimum, your boss's peers might informally sway decisions that affect your growth.

Your boss should not be the only person who is aware of your skills and abilities, this should be aware by management team as well at the same time Don't overlook leaders outside of your company. Even if you're happy in your job, you never know when the Great Reshuffle might lure you to a new opportunity, maintain networks outside your team, company, and industry, to increase your options when it's time for your next move.

"Know Your Customer and Welcome with SWAGAT"

Drive a Culture of Service with (**SWAGAT** - Service with Warmth, Attentiveness, Gratitude, Acknowledge and Trust) across the Organization through own words, action and behavior without compromising Organization Values.

Customer service is not the responsibility of one person, it is the responsibility of every person in Organization.

Make a conscious attempt to understand the stated and unstated needs of the Customer.

Demonstrate Warmth, Attentiveness, Gratitude, Acknowledge and Trust.

Facilitate Teams to analyses various Customer touch points in order to create positive gap between Customer expectation and experience.

If Customer working for Organization like Promoters, it means we correctly welcome to Customer with SWAGAT.

Loyal customers also generate related sales, The profit generated by selling new products and services to existing customers is greater than it is for selling to new customers. The forward-thinking company develops new products by listening to its loyal customers. Loyal customers are therefore more likely to buy because the new product has been designed to meet their needs, and because they have a degree of faith in the company already.

Positive customer referrals are energetic to profit and growth. because satisfied customers are likely to tell 2 other people about a good experience, while dissatisfied customers are likely to tell 10 other people about a bad one.

Not all customers are good customers—in fact, some customers are completely wrong for Organization, Successful companies know exactly who their ideal customers are, and they focus their energy on creating products to please them, and only them.

Change the product not the customer- Once an organization targets its customers and begins to meet and exceed their expectations, customer satisfaction rises. Loyalty follows, bringing with it a significant and measurable impact on the bottom line.

The longer the customer relationship takes, the more profitable it inclines to become, extending the customer relationship from four years to five years resulted in a 30% to 85% increase in profitability.

Please RETAIN Loyal Customer for generate Related Sales and Positive referrals, we must understand Calculation of Customer life time value and Service Profit Chain and always Be ready to Service with SWAGAT beyond frontline.

"Approach An Office Romance - Do's and Don'ts"

Should you date a coworker? Before you act on your feelings, it's important to think through the risks.

Employees spend a lot of time at work and work with each other, talk openly, and romantic relationships are likely to form in such an environment.

The more you get to know that person, the more likely you are to be attracted to each other, and if the situation has come to this point, then you have to take a lot of precautions and you should be aware of the good and bad results.

Aware the Risk Factors

Before you act on your feelings, it's important to think through the risks — and there are quite a few. Of course, there's the chance that the relationship won't work out and that there will be hurt feelings on one or both sides.

If you're dating your teammate, do you put the team's or the individual's interests first? There are also reputational risks. "Your professionalism may be called into question, some colleagues may think you're giving your romantic partner preferential treatment, having a relationship with someone higher up in the organization can create an alternate explanation for why you're succeeding.

intentions matter

If you're aware of these risks and still want to move forward, research shows that your intentions matter. Your coworkers' reactions will reflect what they believe your motives to be, says Baker. When they perceive you as having "ego motive" — seeking out the relationship to serve your own needs, whether it's to get ahead in your company or for your own excitement, check your motives and consider how others will perceive them.

Know Your Organization Policy-POSH

Many companies prohibit employees from dating coworkers, vendors, customers, or suppliers, or require specific disclosures, so be sure to investigate before you start a relationship, follow Organization Policy and check POSH Policy as well.

Stay away from your boss and your subordinates

Whether your intention is good or bad, I believe that stay away from your boss and your subordinates because this is where conflicts of interest are most stark it's important to be open about the relationship with your coworkers and boss, if you don't tell anybody, people will still figure it out, make sure that your manager is one of the first to be informed.

If you break up

Of course, not every romance will work out and if you or your partner decide to end things, it's best to be prepared, If you find it too awkward or painful to continue working alongside the person, you may need to consider leaving the job or at least transferring to another department. No matter how the relationship turns out.

"Pipeline is Lifeline"

"If you not feeding pipeline then it behaves like Rolling Stone"

We have often heard about the pipeline and we have been working on it, this is a very important activity for sales, this is gateway of any business, is means No pipeline No Sales.

Before we can manage the business, we have to learn to manage the pipeline, because the better we manage the pipeline, the better our business will grow.

You will remember that whenever you have missed your target, definitely you having a smaller number of Pipeline Case.

For example, if your Target is 6 Unit then you need to prospect and build at least 10 Pipeline Cases to hit your Target.

Here we will discuss about few Actions and Activity where we can Manage our Pipeline and Business.

Find Enough Opportunity to Hit Target

We have to understand that all pipeline will not mature in Business, at least 30-40% will cancel or postpone for next month therefore initially we have to work on sufficient pipeline cases to hit your Target.

Pipeline just like Roling Stone

Pipeline is just like rolling stone, don't just like Live in, many team members are showing pipeline as Amazing to seniors, don't do this, you have to make conscious attempt to understand the stated and unstated needs of the Customer and act accordingly.

Do not Commit and Celebrate based on Pipeline only

Some salespeople make the mistake of celebrating the opportunity before it becomes a sale, this is situation like to hit an ax in the foot, first work on it and convert in Business then Celebrate the same.

Shape your pipeline up with more than enough opportunities, and then make sure you put in the hard work to close as many of them as you can. It's ok to celebrate creating a new and exciting sales opportunity, but true success comes the moment the deal is closed.

Working and Generating Pipeline in Continuous Process, don't stop it-

As we know Pipeline cases behave like rolling stone then don't stop working and generate it, building pipeline not a day activity it's a 24/7 Activity, All-day, every day, every week, every month, every year, prospecting and building pipeline should never stop if you work in sales, because we know 100% Pipeline not going to convert in Business, you must create a BIG Pool of Pipeline therefore you able to hit your month Target.

Never stop FEEDING your pipeline

Prospect all the time, make it habit, make it a part of your daily routine, because more pipeline more business, keep details of every pipeline case and time to time work on it based on Customer requirement, create such relation with pipeline Customer Whenever the customer has a requirement for your product, the customer just calls you only.

"Corporate Gaslighting"

What is Gaslighting

Gaslighting is meant to foster uncertainty and self-doubt, which is often detrimental to the victim's mental health. Victims of gaslighting may experience anxiety, depression, disorientation, low self-esteem.

It's almost impossible to thrive with a boss who actively undermines your accomplishments, lowers your self-esteem, and hinders your work.

Symptoms of Gaslighting and manipulative boss

Who takes credit for your ideas and hides information.

Who is going out of their way to ensure that you are not developing the skills or experience needed for next role or Promotion.

Who is a master of manipulation, uses reverse psychology to make you feel small and guilty.

who shout, threaten and abuse in meeting and in public.

who know how to fly under the radar.

Who Specializes in undermining an employee's self-esteem, confidence, and sense of reality.

Who blame their mistakes on others.

Who insist that you are incompetent.

Who weaken you in order to control you.

Few Tips and Ways to avoid Gaslighting

Protect your mental health first.

Consider words and actions different from your own.

By reminding yourself that your boss is passive, not you.

Document your conversations.

Be as clear as possible when communicating.

Build relationships with different leaders in your organizations.

Strat exercise, meditate.

Activate your support network and enhance relationship with them.

Surround yourself with friends and people who support and encourage you.

Explain your reasoning and make clear how it will benefit not only you, but your boss and the organization as well.

Find opportunities within your organization.

"Create a Personal Development Plan"

To succeed in professionally and personal life, employees at all levels must learn to identify their weaknesses, uncover their blind spots, and strengthen their skills.

In current scenario employees are changing job very frequently therefore Organization less frequently offers formal training, Organization don't see the value in investing in people who are likely to leave.

Tips to take control of Career Development

first, you all need to understand Job goal, KRA and Success matrix then discuss the same with your reporting boss for their agreement and engage in an ongoing dialogue to ensure you stay on the right track.

Remember TOP Performer always learning and adjusting because Learning is the way of Life, start work on your own KRA and if reporting manager doesn't give you feedback proactively start the conversation yourself because in such situation you have to solve your own blind spots.

Increase your visibility up to the C-suite and become an expert in an area of increasing importance to your company.

"Way to Out of Frying Pan"

some bosses are like this who often tells what's going wrong more than what's going right, working with such critical boss can feel like operating under a microscope.

Meetings sometimes feel like investigations and you spend your days hearing more about what's going wrong than what's going right.

Many assume their manager's negative feedback as a sign that they are incompetent, this couldn't be further from the truth, someone's critical nature has more to do with their own insecurities, bad experiences that have made them overly cautious, or a need to maintain control.

Always take Feedback as Engagement

If your boss is giving you any feedback, so this means that they are paying attention to your work, they want to see you do a better job, they care about you, even if they have a disappointing way of showing it. When you view your manager's criticism as a sign that they're invested in your work, it becomes easier to glean valuable insights from their comments. Their delivery may not be ideal, but they care enough about your development to provide input.

Go beyond their negativity

If you have any Plan for any Task or Project, just explain to your boss before presenting it.

Seeking input early can feel like extra effort, but it shows you understand what's important to your boss, proactively seek their input. is very important Before your boss has a chance to correct you.

Some people naturally have a more negative mindset, and unfortunately, your boss may be one of them, so you may need to push them to see possibilities and investigation for what is working, ask for specific examples and clarification as well.

When your boss gives you feedback that's constructive or even slightly less critical than usual, admit it and sat Thank you for sharing such valuable feedback.

"Are You Planning to Quit Your Job to Start a Business"

60% of young professional's dream of starting their own businesses, it is possible to make the jump from employee to employer, but it's not an easy journey, despite all the publicity about being your own boss, and despite popular success stories, the reality is that more than two-thirds of startups never deliver a positive return to investors. So, before resigning from your job, there are several considerations to bear in mind.

Having a hunger for your product or service will keep you inspired and motivated, even on difficult days when the road ahead looks dark. But passion alone isn't enough. You need to have an exceptional idea that solves a real need in the market by providing unique, competitive, and irreplaceable value.

Before leaving your job build strong network which will help you get your idea off the ground. your network may be your most valuable asset. It will provide you with potential clients, distributors, thought partners, and maybe even investors.

Personal Finance is very important in initial level to run business smoothly and think about how you'll manage your money during the early stages of your business, when income may be less certain, take some time to create a realistic budget that covers your cost of living and the expenditure needed to get your business started.

Businesspersons naturally spend at least half of their time and energy on fundraising, severely limiting the time they have available to focus on other crucial elements of their companies.

You need to be prepared to feel this way, because there will be a boom in business, you will need to work harder, you will be able to work for a longer period of time.

"A Complete Management Epic"

Ramayana is a Sanskrit epic written by Maharishi Valmiki. Friends, this is one of the two huge epics of Indian literature, the other epic being Mahabharata. Ramayana has an important place in Hindu religion in which the duties of relationships have been explained to all of us. There are total about 24,000 verses in Ramayana, all aspects of the human heart have been described in Ramayana. Different situations of life have been depicted by the characters in Ramayana.

Ramayana teaches us how we can lead our life in the right way whether it is personal life or professional life.

It is important to encourage the team

Hanuman ji going to Lanka in search of Goddess Sita is an episode of Ramayana in which the use of management principles is clearly visible. Hanuman ji's aim was to go to Lanka and deliver the message of Shri Ram ji to Goddess Sita, when it was confirmed that Goddess Sita was in Lanka, Jamwant ji inspired Bajrangbali to go to Lanka by making him realize her strength and powers.

Lesson- Jamwant ji motivating Hanuman ji is the best example of a good manager, who introduces his colleagues to their potential. Then helps him to do the work according to his ability.

There are some managers who just tell their employees day and night, nothing is happening, you can't do anything, if it is not happening then resign, just imagine if you tell any employee daily that nothing is happening. Won't be able to So a day will come when the employee will start accepting that he will not be able to do it properly and that employee will lose all his potential.

Assessing Strengths, Weaknesses, Opportunities and Threats

After reaching Lanka, the first thing Hanuman ji did was to completely analyze the situation there. He assessed the strengths and weaknesses of Lanka. In Ravana's territory there were many dangers for him, but there were also many opportunities. Hanuman ji understood everything with his intelligence and skill and then did something.

Lesson- Assessment of Strengths, Weakness, Opportunities and Threats i.e. SWOT (Strength, Weakness, Opportunities and Threats) is the most important part of today's management. First of all, it is important to understand the goal or the work given to you. Then, one has to be mentally prepared for it and make the right plan for it, Last of all, it is important to find out the strengths and weaknesses of your opponent and understand the threats and opportunities related to it.

Work in a planned manner

In Ramayana, Sugriva is shown working in a very planned manner. According to Ramayana, Sugriva possessed the best managerial qualities. His victory in the battle between Sugriva and Bali in Ramayana is a sign of being a successful manager, Seeing the efficiency of Sugriva, Lord Rama acted according to his plan in this war. If Sugriva had been an inefficient manager, perhaps Angad would have been one of his biggest enemies, but Bali's son Angad was with him.

Lesson- It is said that business runs on good relationships. A successful manager is one who has good relations with all his employees and clients. And only a successful manager does good work for his company.

Understanding the importance of coworkers

In Ramayana, as skilled a hero as God was, Ravana was equally bad. From time to time, Ravana showed signs of being an inefficient king, which led to the destruction of his entire empire. From the beginning Ravana ignored the suggestions of his managers and died in battle with Rama.

There are some managers who repeatedly ignore the market and industry feedback given by their employees and keep doing it with their own people, even if the business gets destroyed and the entire team resigns. Why not do it, in such a situation his condition also becomes like Ravana.

Before the kidnapping of Mother Sita, Marich had tried his best to understand Ravana and said that such a king is not ready to give consent to his well-wishers. We call him self-willed and ultimately leads to destruction. Have your wise ministers discussed this issue? did not give you any consent.

Lesson- A good manager is one who can outwork his competitors. Because he also listens and implements the suggestions of the people working with him. Especially when the company needs them the most but it was Ravana's mismanagement due to which Vibhishana, the most intelligent and skilled commander of his army, left him in the middle of the war and joined Lord Rama.

A team leader should create more leaders

After finding Mother Sita in Lanka, Hanuman ji, as per his wish, burnt Ravana's golden Lanka to ashes. But Lord Ram was very sad with this decision of Hanuman ji. After which Hanuman ji stopped taking any kind of decisions, to improve Hanuman ji's decision making abilities, Ram ji had to remove himself from the entire scenario.

During the war, Ravana kidnapped Lord Ram and Lakshman and took them to the underworld. Only Hanuman ji had the intellectual and physical strength to save him. It was Hanuman ji who saved Ram and Lakshman from the clutches of evil Ravana. And Hanuman ji realized his powers and Hanuman ji was able to become a successful hero.

Lesson-Similarly, in the corporate world too, a leader faces a time when he has to prepare many other leaders like him. The biggest task in this is to inspire the people working around you to take good and successful decisions so that in future they too can become good managers.

Preparing a Successor

King Dasharatha wanted Ram ji to sit on the throne of Ayodhya, but this could not happen. Being the eldest son, the people had already accepted Ram ji as their king. And when Ram ji returned to Ayodhya after completing his exile, then he was the one who took charge of the kingdom. And learning from this, Ram ji divided the kingdom equally between his two sons Luv and Kush.

Lesson- Similarly, all well-managed companies ensure that planning for the careers and future development of their top performers is directly linked to succession planning Therefore, good leaders should always help in enhancing and honing the skills of their team's best performers, so that the company does not suffer any loss in their absence.

Understanding Consumer Needs

When Ram ji was sent into exile for 14 years, Goddess Sita and Anuj Lakshman also decided to go with him. He accepted this opportunity as a challenge. He did this because he also wanted to understand life by living with the common people like them. For this he gave up luxuries.

Lesson- Even in modern marketing today, executives first meet people to understand the needs of the consumer. Understand their thoughts and experiences. After that the product is made as per the need of the consumer.

Excellence in Execution

Hanuman ji had implemented the plan to search for Mother Sita. The cleverness and knowledge with which he searches for Sita ji and reaches his goal is an example of a successful and intelligent hero. While crossing the sea, he rejected the offer of a short rest by Mount Mainak.

Lesson- The way Hanuman ji had ensured that he would locate Mother Sita. In the same way, a manager should first fulfill his target and then think about taking rest.

Recognition of Right and Wrong

Ravana in Ramayana was such a personality from whom a lot can be learned. Like when Ravana's wife Mandodari, brother Vibhishan and grandfather asked him to return Goddess Sita to Ram ji, but in his arrogance, he did not listen to them, He listened to those who were instigating him against Lord Rama. And this became the reason for his destruction.

Lesson- Even today some people are busy in spoiling the work done in their ego and just keep eating. For them, the end of Ravana is the biggest lesson, there are some managers who make the policy wrong knowingly or unknowingly, but such managers put pressure on the team to implement the policy instead of improving it, and they try to prove the policy right and give ground information about their team but also ignore it, which ruins everything, including the business and the team's confidence.

Setting a Goal

Lord Ram's goal was to save his wife Sita and destroy the evil ones. And he had instilled the same goal in his army that the purpose of the war was to free Goddess Sita from the captivity of Ravana.

Lesson-Even in the corporate world today, every person in the company should focus on his or her set goal. If all the people working from bottom to top positions achieve their respective goals, then no one can stop the company from reaching the top.

Excellent Management

One of the most obvious incidents, in which management is very clearly visible, is Hanuman ji's visit to Lanka. His mission there was to locate Sita Mata and give her the message of Lord Rama. When it became clear that Sita ji was in Lanka, Jamwant asked Hanuman to go there, He helped Hanuman ji realize his true potential and inspired him to go to the enemy stronghold i.e. Lanka.

Lesson

Jamwant motivating Hanuman is an excellent example of a good manager helping his employees realize their potential and perform to their potential.

Hanuman Analysis

Once mentally prepared for the job, the first thing Hanuman did after reaching Lanka was to conduct a thorough analysis of the situation. He made a thorough study of the Lankans, assessing their strengths and weaknesses, the various threats and opportunities present in the enemy camp.

Lesson

SWOT (Strengths, Weaknesses, Opportunities and Threats) analysis is one of the most important aspects of management today. First you have to figure out the goal, or the task to be done. Then, prepare mentally for it and make a perfect plan and then, analyze the competitor's strengths and weaknesses and what threats and opportunities are at work. Hanuman ji also did the same after reaching Lanka due to which he got success in his work. You cannot do anything properly without preparation and planning.

Definitely form an Alliance

Sugriva has shown some excellent managerial qualities in Ramayana. As a successful manager, he got Rama to do his bidding and got his kingdom back from a brother who was much more powerful than him, using his managerial skills he also hired Angad to work for him. If Sugriva had been a bad manager, Angad would have become his staunch enemy.

Lesson

It is said that business runs on relationships. A manager who can build good relationships with employees, customers, etc. can-do wonders for his company. Lord Ram was very good at this. He was an expert in maintaining relationships, His skill in this was so great that even when Ravana was lying injured on the battlefield and about to die, he sent Lakshmana to take from him some important lessons which he had learned in his life.

Value your Subordinates

In the same Ramayana, Ravana has repeatedly shown traits of a bad manager, which led to the end of his kingdom. From the beginning he ignored the suggestions of his managers.

Lesson

A good manager is one who can get his work done even by his competitors. A good manager listens to his subordinates and tries to keep them united, especially when the organization needs them most.

But due to Ravana's mismanagement, Vibhishana, his brother, also decided to leave Ravana amid the crisis.

Nothing is bigger than Brand

In the Ramayana, in the sequence of building a bridge to Lanka, when the stones were being immersed in water, the name of Ram was written on the stones, after which even the heavy and big stones started floating on the water. And in a relatively short time the bridge to Lanka was ready. After this it was said that there is no name bigger than the name of Ram.

Lesson-The stones were sinking because the name Ram was not engraved on them. If seen in today's time, the name of the brand prevails in the market and the name of the brand owner is not bigger than the brand. Any manager is very happy when he is recognized by the name of his company.

Importance of Communication

According to Ramayana, when Sugriva saw that while fighting the demon, Bali went into a cave and neither the demon nor Bali came out for 1 year, Sugriva thought that perhaps both of them had killed each other. And after coming back to his kingdom Kishkindha, Sugriva married Bali's wife Tara.

When Bali returned, he saw Sugriva sitting on the throne and thought that he had been cheated. And he challenged Sugriva for war without talking or understanding. Here, the reason for the deadly enmity between two brothers Sugriva and Bali was not talking to each other.

Lesson- Miscommunication of any kind should never be allowed in any kind of management and control, otherwise the results are opposite to the expected. Therefore, a manager should always keep talking with his employees.

You said to the strangers, we heard from the strangers, you must have told something to us too, you must have heard something from us also.

It is important to have confidence in the Team

In Ramayana, the army of demons was not more powerful than the army of the gods, but still they defeated the gods and powerful kings. At the same time, Lord Ram's army consisted of soldiers who belonged to tribal tribes, who had never faced such a powerful and sophisticated army before Despite this, Ram ji had full faith in his army. He knew everything about the capabilities of his army. And due to this confidence, the monkey army overpowered Ravana's powerful army and won.

Lesson-The lesson to be learned from this is to first set ambitious goals and then motivate your team to reach that goal and not keep saying daily you can't do it.

"Pulse Check"

The transition from college to the corporate world isn't always smooth sailing. The cultural shift can be overwhelming.

You studied and worked hard, got your degree, and secured a full-time job, Congratulations! You're onto the next stage of maturity: building your career.

After onboarding first 100 Days is very crucial for both Employee, Reporting Manager and Employer.

Welcome to your first 100 Days in the corporate world. This job will be a entrance to future opportunities. Here's how to get off to a strong start.

For Employee

Get to know your company. Even if you enclosed a lot during your interview, I recommend doing a more in-depth investigation prior to your first day of work. Set up news alerts about your company and follow social media page to stay updated.

in initial days you have to follow concept WLL (Watch, Listen, Learn) very carefully.

watch the important activity like how do other employee prefer for Communication in person or email, which behaviour are rewarded.

There are a few habits you may have to adjust. Ask questions — a lot of them. You need to ask questions to learn the basics of how your team and larger organization function.

spend time documenting what you've learned to help you reflect, process, and retain any important lessons. Build a positive relationship with your boss because Your boss may be the single most important person in your new job, pay attention to how your boss interacts with yourself and others.

Your boss will also be a great resource to you as you start to build relationships and understand who holds the decision-making power at your company. They're your gateway to other influential leaders and can help you expand your internal network.

Accept a growth mindset. A growth mindset is the belief that you can change and grow through effort and experience.

For Reporting Manager / Employer

First 100 Days is very important for New Join employee, here Manager Role are very crucial and handholding to Team like new born baby.

Just like a newborn is examined by a doctor to assess health, a new employee goes through an onboarding process to understand their skills, strengths, and areas needing further development.

Maintaining a consistent temperature and comfortable surroundings for a baby mirror providing a clear work structure, defined roles, and supportive team dynamics for a new employee.

For new born baby ensuring proper feeding, warmth, hygiene, and bonding, while for a new employee, it means clear expectations, introductions to key people, training on core processes, and regular check-ins to gauge adaptation and identify any potential challenges.

"Presentation Always Matter"

It is very important to be full of confidence during the presentation, only then we are able to present our point with full confidence and attract the attention of the listener. During the presentation, we should take some precautions and control some body movements. should take into account Body language is very important during presentation and by keeping some important things in mind to control it, we can present our point in the best way.

Visualizing box size during presentation

During the presentation, you have to imagine that there is a box in front of your chest and stomach and you are incorporating the movements of your hands inside the box, this action will help you to control your body language and you will be able to speak during the presentation. will be full of confidence.

Visualizing catching a ball during a presentation

During a presentation, gesture as if you are holding a basketball between your hands, this position shows confidence and control, as if you have the facts in your hands.

Pyramid hand/vertical fingers

Holding your hands upward, slightly opened and fingers touching (in front of your body), to form a tower or pyramid, displays confidence for example, a downward gesture with your arms and hands on the table shows that you are focused and listening to the speaker.

broad stance

How people stand is a strong indicator of their mindset. When you stand in this strong and stable position, your feet are approximately shoulder-width apart, indicating that you feel in control.

The next time you give a presentation, try recording it, then review the video with the sound off and just watching your body language. How did you stand and gesture? Have you used any of these terms, if not, think about how you can do this the next time you're in front of an audience, or even talking to your boss or a big client. Practice in front of a mirror, then with friends, until they feel natural.

"The Corporate Barrier"

In today's fast-paced business world, innovation is the lifeblood of success, Yet, a pervasive problem lurks within many organizations: managers often overlook or ignore valuable ideas from their employees Whereas employee ideas are gold mines of potential growth and improvement.

The structures and cultures meant to simplify smooth operations often become barriers, creating invisible walls that block the flow of ideas from the ground up.

We will talk about some such invisible walls which hinder the growth of the organization and its direct impact is on the employees.

The Hierarchical Barrier

Visualize a fortress where ideas are stuck at the bottom, unable to scale the steep walls of corporate hierarchy. This is the reality in many organizations where traditional top-down structures reign supreme. In these situations, the unspoken rule is clear: innovation flows from the top, wisdom resides in the corner offices, and employees are mere executors of pre-determined strategies.

In such scenario not only discourages employees from sharing ideas but also supports the dangerous perception that management holds a monopoly on innovation, A stifling atmosphere where potential breakthroughs are silenced before they can even echo through the organizational ranks.

In such an environment, even if the employee has good ideas, he will not share them, and gradually all the innovation and creativity of the employee will end and this has a direct impact on the performance of the employee and the organization.

The Cultural Barrier

Sometimes corporate culture act as an invisible barrier to innovation and new ideas are seen as threats rather than opportunities The notorious "Not Invented Here" syndrome plagues many organizations, where ideas originating by employee are instinctively rejected.

This cultural resistance creates a environment where employees learn that it's safer to conform than to innovate that is very harmful for Organization and badly impacting on employees career growth.

The Bias Barrier

Unconscious biases permeate organizations, creating subtle but significant barriers to innovation.

Ideas from certain departments or lower hierarchical levels often face unwarranted, regardless of their merit, confirmation bias often leads managers to Favor ideas that align with their existing beliefs or strategies, blinding them to potentially groundbreaking but unconventional suggestions. This bias wall not only limits the pool of ideas considered but also reinforces existing power structures and thought patterns, stifling the diversity of thought essential for true innovation.

Sometimes, due to personal bias, people consider themselves to be the most knowledgeable person and consider themselves superior to the creator of this universe as well, and such an employee gets filled with ego and the ghost of Pushpa Movie dialogue "Jhukega Nahi" gets ingrained in them Such managers become so prejudiced that they know even before the interview which candidate will do well and which will not.

The Bureaucracy Barrier

In many organizations, the very systems designed to ensure efficiency and consistency become barriers to innovation. Excessive red tape, lengthy approval processes, and rigid protocols create a bureaucratic maze that ideas must navigate to reach implementation. This bureaucratic wall is particularly daunting for employees whose innovative ideas challenge existing processes or cross departmental boundaries.

The Results-Only Barrier

A culture that rewards only for results while ignoring the effort and learning involved in innovation creates a formidable barrier to idea generation and sharing.

When employees know they'll be judged solely on the success or failure of their ideas, not on the valuable insights gained from the process, they're less likely to propose novel solutions, this wall creates a fear-driven environment were playing it safe is preferable to pushing boundaries, ultimately stifling the creative spirit essential for organizational growth and adaptation.

Dismantling these barriers requires a multifaceted approach that addresses both structural and cultural elements of the organization. Companies must foster an environment where ideas can flow freely across hierarchical levels, departments, and teams. This involves creating safe spaces for idea sharing, implementing transparent feedback mechanisms, and recognizing both the effort and outcomes of innovation attempts.

"Lord Shri Ram-The Ultimate Dealership"

We all must have read and heard Ramayana, a very beautiful incident happened, many difficulties came in the life of Lord Shri Ram, he is a king, for some reason he has to leave his kingdom, or he abandons it, he was so gentle. that he did not oppose it at all, and they go and live in the forest and live a life full of troubles, during this many incidents happen, Ravana kidnaps Mother Sita and Lord Shri Ram's love for Mother Sita and the pain caused by this incident and what happens to them. Worried about what is happening, they go to South India and They gather an army there and go to Sri Lanka and fight a war, kill Ravana in the war, as we know Ravana had ten heads and here, we are so troubled by only one head, Lord Shri Ram had to kill Ravana ten times to kill him completely, Lord Shri Ram won the war and is returning to Ayodhya.

Lord Shri Ram decides that I do not want to go back to Ayodhya but I want to go to the Himalayas and spend some time in the cave of Agatsya Muni, so that I can atone for the sins committed by me, I have killed a person who was a devotee of Lord Shiva and a religious person, a great scholar and a great king. The rest of the people were surprised to hear the words of Lord Shri Ram. Lakshman ji said, what are you talking about, Ravana. had kidnapped Mother Sita, how can you think like this about him, Lord Shri Ram said, that was the work of the other nine heads, Ravana's nine heads were filled with greed, anger, ego, lust etc. but his one head was filled with knowledge, wisdom, righteousness and devotion. and i regret cutting that head off.

If I had my way, I would not have cut off that head and would not have killed Ravana, but it was not possible to do so, so I had to kill him, but now I am very regretful about cutting off that one head.

In this case one is trying to tell that we all have ten or more heads, have we noticed that someday in the head there is greed, hatred, jealousy, love or beauty or maybe we all in the same days. We go through things, we will say what we see the moment we see it, There are different heads working at different times but in all of them there is a head in each of them which is of love, goodwill, compassion and generosity, The biggest mistake we make in our life is that instead of recognizing and criticizing a person, we start criticizing that person, Lord Shri Ram is trying to say that Ravana did a lot of wrong things but he did not do anything to others. There were nine heads but I saw a lot of good things in one head, this is a basic rule and we all should follow it, if we see something wrong in any person then we should only criticize that mistake and not that person, when we do the same with others then the same will happen with us too. will be, If we do not strengthen the potential and remove that which acts as a hindrance to the potential, then we are not spiritual seekers. A rose plant has more thorns than flowers, yet it is called a rose, because we recognize beauty, Similarly, a mango tree has more leaves than fruits, we also call it a mango tree and not a tree of leaves, similarly we should see this in people, we should see in all the people around us whether we are can recognize a drop of sweetness, Because if we do not recognize it, it will not appear within us, it does not mean that we should turn a blind eye to everything, we see thorns and leaves but we recognize flowers and fruits.

"Salute to Field Force"

First of all, Salute to all B Players for their Selfless and Dedication towards responsibility, at the same time request to all Seniors or Management to Stop underestimating your B players.

We must retain support and motivate to them to reach their Potential.

Please remember B Players are often less concerned about their personal path and are more likely to beyond in order to support customers, colleagues, and the reputation of the business.

You have to identify the strengths of each Team member and first things to do is we must have good knowledge about B Players one to one, few players get their task done but never speak up in crowd, can often be overlooked when it comes to leadership roles. Unlock any hidden potential by asking them about their concerns, their preferences and their ideas.

After knowing strengths of individuals, you can assess whether people are in the best place or with right job then take corrective step accordingly.

Sometimes B Players have doubts about their own ability to step up on A Role, here your role should be Identify, appreciate and give appropriate handholding and coaching to those who have skills but not the confidence to make that leap.

Demonstrate your consent for them to assume control. B players may be reticent until they have clear permission from you.

"Actionable Tips for Managing Underperformance"

Underperform on occasionally is normal things, in such situation avoid becoming defensive or emotional, just stay calm don't blame or shame yourself, be professional.

In this situation your first step should be identify the problem and try to figure out what's causing the issue, sometime our effort doesn't immediate translate into expected organization outcomes, irrespective you are doing right things but unfortunately it taking long time lead to positive result.

The same time you think about your underperformance from your Boss perspective and think about reaction of Boss.

Instead Blame or shame yourself, Focused on Correction and way forward.

Acknowledge your mistake and express regret, Take Ownership and move forward with Responsibility.

Think about what you want to achieve and support required from Management.

Explain your plan and idea to Boss that how you are going to improve situation and request your Boss for guidance, Effective communication can help you build a good relationship with your Boss.

Your underperformance might also be a sign that you need to find a position at your company that's better suited to your strengths, take feedback or advice from your Boss and Team HR for identifying and transitioning to a more suitable role.

"Balance Emotional Insight"

I have heard Sadhguru ji saying that only two voices come from the heart, Loved Up, all the rest of the voices come from your mind, some things of this thought come from the heart and some from the mind, this is just an analogy.

The heart is a simple pump. Don't give it any other responsibility except to pump blood continuously and keep you alive, unless someone breaks it.

The brain is a new device that you have got in the process of evolution. This much development of the brain has happened a short time ago. In comparison to other systems, if you dissect any mammal, then all of them have all these parts, whatever organs you have, they have them. is also Even if you bite a frog, there is a big difference in whatever is in you too. The debate is about the development of the brain which has happened recently, because of it being so recent, most of the people have not been able to understand how to handle it,

So, the operating instructions are very important, the operating instructions are not read when it is time to throw away the machine, you teach it within the first few days, if you buy a new phone then you learn how to operate it in the first 3-5 days. Would you like to learn it in 2016 or after 3 years when you are about to throw it away, It has never happened that the heart has generated any thought or purpose, yes when you have seen a young girl or boy, the heart starts beating more, it does not mean that he is saying anything, it is just due to other excitements. Managing the shortage the heart is not trying to say anything, it is just filling the gap. If you want more blood, then it is pumping a little faster. This also happens when you climb stairs, just as you feel short of breath when you are in love, similarly when you climb stairs. also flourishes.

This happens to many people even when they are stressed, so the heart is not trying to say anything, it is just trying to ensure that blood reaches every part of the body. If this is your brain, then it is speaking in different languages. Yes, as thoughts arise, so do emotions arise.

Thank You

Corporate sector has an invaluable contribution to society and the nation. Their tireless efforts to drive economic growth, promote social welfare, and protect the environment have made a profound impact on our lives.

commitment of corporate social responsibility, which has led to numerous initiatives that benefit local communities, support education and healthcare, and promote environmental sustainability. The philanthropic efforts have touched the lives of millions, providing hope and opportunities for a better future.

We must acknowledge their role in driving innovation and technological advancements, which have transformed industries and improved the quality of life for citizens. investments in research and development have led to breakthroughs in fields such as healthcare, renewable energy, and transportation.

Corporate contributions to the nation's economic growth, which have created jobs, stimulated economic activity, and generated revenue. Their investments in infrastructure development have supported the construction of critical infrastructure, including roads, bridges, and public transportation systems.

Corporates made significant difference in the lives of citizens, and we look forward to your continued contributions to building a better future for all.

Special Thanks to my Best Friend Mr. Ravi Shankar Jyoti who always guide and support me on my Career Path.

Dear Family / Friends "I'm so thankful for your support and the way you always have my back.

Upcoming Book...

www.ingramcontent.com/pod-product-compliance
Lightning Source LLC
Chambersburg PA
CBHW031305130726
47988CB00007B/2744